Mastering PC & Laptop Repair:

A Comprehensive Guide

Atif Shahzad Khan

Atif Shahzad Khan

Atif Shahzad Khan

Chapter 5: Hardware Replacement and Upgrades

- Replacing RAM and Storage
- Installing Graphics Cards
- Upgrading CPUs

Chapter 6: Preventative Maintenance

- Cleaning and Dust Removal
- Cooling System Maintenance

Chapter 7: Operating System Installation and Optimization

- Installing Windows, macOS, or Linux
- System Optimization Tips

Chapter 8: Data Backup and Recovery

- Backup Strategies
- Data Recovery Methods

Chapter 9: Networking and Internet Connectivity

- Troubleshooting Network Issues
- Wi-Fi Setup and Security

Chapter 10: Laptop-Specific Repairs

- Screen Replacement
- Battery Replacement
- Keyboard and Touchpad Repairs

Atif Shahzad Khan

Chapter 11: Advanced Troubleshooting Techniques

- BIOS/UEFI Configuration
- Dealing with Boot Problems

Chapter 12: Resources and References

- Useful Websites and Forums
- Recommended Books and Courses

Chapter 13: Virus and Malware Removal

- Identifying and Removing Malware
- Tips for Preventing Infections

Chapter 14: Data Security and Privacy

- Importance of Data Security
- Encrypting Your Data
- Secure Data Disposal

Chapter 15: Troubleshooting Specific Error Messages

- Common Error Messages and Their Solutions

Chapter 16: BIOS/UEFI and Firmware Updates

- Updating Motherboard Firmware
- Importance of Keeping Firmware Updated

Atif Shahzad Khan

Chapter 17: Hardware Testing and Diagnostics

- Using Diagnostic Tools
- Stress Testing Components

Chapter 18: Soldering and Component-Level Repairs

- Introduction to Soldering
- Repairing Circuit Boards

Chapter 19: Overheating and Cooling Solutions

- Diagnosing Overheating Issues
- Advanced Cooling Solutions

Chapter 20: Warranty, Repair Services, and DIY

- Understanding Manufacturer Warranties
- When to Seek Professional Repair Services

Chapter 21: Troubleshooting Specific Laptop Brands and Models

- Tips for Repairing Popular Laptop Brands
- Resources for Specific Models

Chapter 22: Building Your Own PC

- Custom PC Building Guide
- Choosing Compatible Components

Atif Shahzad Khan

Chapter 23: Future Trends in PC and Laptop Repair

- Emerging Technologies and Repair Challenges

Chapter 24: Troubleshooting Resources and Tools

- A Detailed List of Useful Resources and Tools

Chapter 25: Real-Life Repair Stories and Case Studies

- Stories of Successful Repairs
- Lessons Learned from Repairing PCs and Laptops

Chapter 26: Reader's Q&A and Troubleshooting Solutions

- Answering Common Questions from Readers
- Sharing Reader Success Stories

Chapter 27: Additional Tips and Tricks

- Time-Saving Techniques
- Maximizing Efficiency in Repairs

Chapter 28: Building a PC Repair Business

- Tips for Starting a PC Repair Business
- Marketing and Customer Relations

Atif Shahzad Khan

Conclusion

- Final Thoughts and Encouragement
- Encouraging Readers to Continue Learning and Exploring
- Recap of Key Points
- Encouragement for Readers

Appendix

- Glossary of Technical Terms
- Troubleshooting Flowcharts
- Quick Reference Guides

Atif Shahzad Khan

About The Author

Atif Shahzad Khan

Hi, I'm Atif Shahzad Khan, and I have a background in computer science and a passion for helping people to give knowledge about computer network systems, cybersecurity, network security, self security in cyber world and much more. With over a decade of experience in the industry, I've worked with clients from all walks of life and understand the unique challenges faced by underrepresented communities. Through my work as a computer science engineer, I strive to create more equitable access to computer education and resources. I'm thrilled to be a author of this ebook, and to share my perspective and expertise with everyone.

Atif Shahzad Khan

Copyright

Atif Shahzad Khan

Dedication

To my loving parents,

Who filled my life with wisdom, love, and unwavering support. Your guidance and encouragement have been the cornerstone of my journey.

To my loving siblings,

Whose laughter, camaraderie, and shared experiences have made life brighter and richer. Together, we've created cherished memories that will last a lifetime.

To my lovely beautiful wife,

Whose presence has brought boundless joy and warmth into my world. Your love is my greatest treasure, and our journey together is a source of endless happiness.

To my cute lovely child,

Whose innocence, curiosity, and endless wonder inspire me every day. You are the future, and I'm committed to creating a world where your dreams can flourish.

This book is dedicated to all of you, my pillars of strength, my endless source of love, and my greatest blessings. Your unwavering support and love have fueled my passions and dreams. With heartfelt gratitude, this book is for you.

With all my love,

Atif Shahzad Khan

Introduction

In an age dominated by technology, our reliance on personal computers and laptops has grown exponentially. These devices are our digital companions, serving as tools for work, communication, entertainment, and beyond. However, like any complex machinery, they are not immune to issues and malfunctions.

Learning how to repair PCs and laptops is not just a valuable skill; it's a practical necessity in today's world. In this comprehensive guide, we'll delve into the art of troubleshooting, diagnosing, and fixing common problems that can plague your machines.

Why Learn PC & Laptop Repair

1. Empowerment: Have you ever felt helpless when your computer suddenly crashes, or your laptop refuses to boot up? By mastering PC and laptop repair, you gain a sense of control over these situations. No longer will you need to rely solely on costly tech support or extended downtime. Instead, you can take matters into your own hands.

2. Cost Savings: Professional repairs can be expensive, often involving not only service fees but also parts replacement costs. By learning to repair your devices, you'll save a substantial amount of money over time. Your wallet will thank you, and you'll have more resources for the things that matter most to you.

Atif Shahzad Khan

3. Sustainability: As our world becomes more environmentally conscious, knowing how to repair and maintain your devices contributes to a sustainable lifestyle. Extending the lifespan of your PC or laptop reduces electronic waste, which is a growing concern in our throwaway culture.

Importance of DIY Repair

1. Self-Sufficiency: DIY repair not only saves you money but also empowers you to become self-sufficient. You'll no longer need to wait for a technician or endure the inconvenience of not having your device when you need it most.

2. Learning and Growth: Engaging in DIY repair fosters a sense of curiosity and continuous learning. You'll delve into the inner workings of technology, expanding your knowledge and problem-solving skills.

3. Customization: Repairing your devices allows you to customize and upgrade them according to your needs. You can choose the components that suit your preferences and optimize your machine for peak performance.

Safety Precautions

1. Protecting Yourself: Safety should always be a priority when working with electronic devices. In this guide, we'll emphasize safety measures such as proper handling of electrical components, safe disassembly procedures, and protection against electrical hazards.

Atif Shahzad Khan

2. Data Security: We'll also address the importance of safeguarding your data during repair. You'll learn how to protect your valuable information from accidental loss or exposure.

By embarking on this journey to mastering PC and laptop repair, you're taking the first step towards a more empowered, cost-effective, and environmentally conscious tech-savvy lifestyle. In the following chapters, we'll equip you with the knowledge, skills, and confidence needed to tackle a wide range of issues and ensure your devices serve you reliably for years to come.

Atif Shahzad Khan

Chapter 1: Understanding PC and Laptop Hardware

Before you can effectively repair and maintain PCs and laptops, it's crucial to have a solid understanding of the hardware that makes up these devices. In this chapter, we'll delve into the components that constitute a PC and laptop and familiarize you with basic hardware terminology. This knowledge will serve as the foundation for your journey into the world of tech repair.

Components of a PC and Laptop

1. Central Processing Unit (CPU)

The CPU, often referred to as the brain of the computer, performs calculations and executes instructions. It's a critical component for the device's overall performance.

2. Motherboard

The motherboard serves as the main circuit board, connecting all the hardware components. It houses the CPU, RAM slots, and various ports for connecting peripherals.

3. Random Access Memory (RAM)

RAM is the computer's short-term memory. It stores data and programs that are actively being used, allowing for quick access by the CPU. Upgrading RAM can improve system performance.

Atif Shahzad Khan

4. Storage Devices

Laptops and PCs use various storage devices, including Hard Disk Drives (HDDs) and Solid-State Drives (SSDs), to store data and the operating system. Understanding storage types is crucial for upgrades and data recovery.

5. Power Supply Unit (PSU)

The PSU converts electrical energy from the outlet into the voltage and current needed to power the components. It's a vital part of the computer's functionality.

6. Graphics Processing Unit (GPU)

The GPU, also known as the graphics card, handles rendering and display tasks. In laptops, it may be integrated into the motherboard, while desktop PCs often have dedicated GPUs.

7. Input and Output Ports

These include USB ports, audio jacks, HDMI, VGA, and more. They facilitate connections to peripherals like keyboards, mice, monitors, and external storage devices.

8. Cooling System

Laptops and PCs require cooling to prevent overheating. This system typically includes fans, heat sinks, and thermal paste to dissipate heat generated by the CPU and GPU.

9. Optical Drive

Optical drives like CD/DVD-ROM or Blu-ray drives, though less common today, are still present in some laptops and desktops for reading and writing optical discs.

Basic Hardware Terminology

1. Hardware

Hardware refers to the physical components of a computer, such as the CPU, RAM, motherboard, and storage devices. It's tangible and can be touched.

2. Software

Software encompasses the programs, applications, and operating system that run on the hardware. Unlike hardware, it's intangible and consists of code and data.

3. BIOS/UEFI

The Basic Input/Output System (BIOS) or Unified Extensible Firmware Interface (UEFI) is firmware that initializes hardware components during startup and facilitates communication between the hardware and software.

4. Peripheral

Peripherals are external devices connected to the computer, including keyboards, mice, printers, and monitors.

5. Driver

Drivers are software programs that allow the operating system to communicate with and control hardware devices effectively. Installing the right drivers is crucial for hardware functionality.

6. Expansion Slot

Expansion slots on the motherboard allow you to add additional hardware components like graphics cards, sound cards, and network cards.

7. Bus

A bus is a communication pathway that allows data and instructions to flow between hardware components, such as the CPU and RAM.

In this chapter, we've introduced you to the fundamental components of PCs and laptops and provided key hardware terminology. Building a strong foundation in hardware knowledge is essential as you embark on your journey to master PC and laptop repair. In the subsequent chapters, we'll dive deeper into troubleshooting and repair techniques to help you become a proficient tech repair enthusiast.

Chapter 2: Tools and Equipment

In the world of PC and laptop repair, having the right tools and equipment is paramount. Whether you're replacing a faulty component, diagnosing a software issue, or conducting routine maintenance, having a well-equipped toolbox is your first step toward successful repairs. In this chapter, we'll delve into the essential tools for repair and discuss the importance of safety gear in ensuring both your well-being and the longevity of your devices.

Essential Tools for Repair

Screwdrivers

One of the most basic but crucial tools in your arsenal is the screwdriver. These come in various types and sizes, including Phillips, flathead, Torx, and more. Different devices may require different screwdriver types, so it's essential to have a comprehensive set.

Pliers and Tweezers

Precision handling is often needed when dealing with small components and delicate connections. Pliers and tweezers are invaluable for grasping, bending, or holding tiny parts without causing damage.

Spudgers and Plastic Opening Tools

When disassembling devices, especially laptops and smartphones, you'll want to avoid scratching or damaging the

Atif Shahzad Khan

casing. Spudgers and plastic opening tools are designed for prying open cases and separating components safely.

Multimeter

For diagnosing electrical issues, a multimeter is indispensable. It allows you to test voltage, continuity, and resistance, helping you pinpoint problems in power supplies, circuitry, and components.

Anti-static Wrist Strap

Electrostatic discharge (ESD) can harm sensitive electronic components. An anti-static wrist strap, when properly grounded, prevents the buildup of static electricity in your body, safeguarding your components from ESD damage.

Heat Gun or Soldering Iron

Advanced repairs, such as soldering components or reflowing solder joints, require specialized tools like a soldering iron or heat gun. These tools are essential for intricate hardware fixes.

Cable Ties, Tape, and Adhesives

Securing loose cables, taping down wires, and using adhesives when necessary are essential for keeping components and connections in place during and after repairs.

Magnifying Glass or Loupe

Enhance your visibility during detailed work by using a magnifying glass or loupe. This can help you identify tiny components and inspect solder joints with precision.

Tool Organization

Maintaining an organized workspace is critical. Toolboxes, organizers, and labeled containers can help you keep your tools and equipment orderly, making it easier to locate what you need when you need it.

Safety Gear

While tools enable you to perform repairs, safety gear ensures you do so without compromising your well-being. Here's a rundown of essential safety gear:

Safety Glasses

Protect your eyes from flying debris, sparks, and dust by wearing safety glasses. Eye protection is non-negotiable when working with tools.

Gloves

Quality work gloves shield your hands from sharp edges, heat, and chemicals. Choose gloves suitable for the specific task to ensure maximum protection.

Atif Shahzad Khan

Respirator Mask

When working with materials that produce dust or fumes, a respirator mask helps prevent inhalation of harmful particles, ensuring your respiratory health.

Ear Protection

Protracted exposure to noisy components, such as cooling fans or power tools, can lead to hearing damage. Ear protection, like earplugs or earmuffs, reduces noise-related stress on your ears.

Ergonomic Tools and Workspace

To prevent repetitive stress injuries (RSIs) like carpal tunnel syndrome, choose ergonomic tools designed to reduce strain on your wrists and hands. Additionally, set up an ergonomic workspace with an adjustable chair and proper lighting to support your comfort and posture.

In this chapter, we've laid the foundation for your journey into PC and laptop repair by introducing the essential tools and safety gear you'll need. Armed with this knowledge and the right equipment, you'll be ready to tackle a wide range of repairs confidently and safely. As we progress through the guide, you'll learn how to put these tools and safety measures into practice effectively.

Atif Shahzad Khan

Chapter 3: Diagnosing Common Issues

In this chapter, we'll equip you with the essential skills for diagnosing common issues that plague PCs and laptops. Effective troubleshooting techniques and the ability to distinguish between hardware and software problems are invaluable in the repair process. By the end of this chapter, you'll have a clear understanding of how to pinpoint and assess issues with your devices.

Troubleshooting Techniques

1. Observation

Begin by observing the problem closely. Pay attention to error messages, unusual sounds, or unexpected behavior. Note any recent changes or events that might be related to the issue.

2. Rebooting

Sometimes, issues can be resolved with a simple reboot. Restarting your computer or laptop can clear temporary glitches in software and hardware.

3. Isolation

Isolate the problem by determining if it's related to hardware or software. Try running different programs or performing various tasks to see if the issue persists.

Atif Shahzad Khan

4. Research

Consult online resources, forums, and user manuals to see if others have experienced similar problems. This can provide valuable insights and potential solutions.

5. Testing

Use diagnostic tools to test hardware components like the CPU, RAM, and storage devices. These tests can help identify failing hardware.

6. Safe Mode

Booting your computer or laptop into safe mode can help determine if a software application or driver is causing the issue. Safe mode loads only essential system files.

7. Event Logs

Check system and application event logs for error messages and warnings. These logs can provide clues about what went wrong.

8. External Devices

Disconnect external devices and peripherals to rule out compatibility issues or faulty hardware. Sometimes, a malfunctioning external device can disrupt your computer's operation.

Identifying Hardware and Software Problems

Hardware Problems

1. Common Hardware Issues

- **Overheating:** Computers and laptops can overheat due to dust accumulation or a malfunctioning cooling system. Symptoms include frequent crashes or shutdowns.
- **Faulty RAM:** Insufficient RAM or defective memory modules can lead to system instability, crashes, or the "Blue Screen of Death" (BSOD).
- **Hard Drive Failure:** Symptoms include slow performance, data corruption, or unusual noises from the hard drive.
- **Graphics Card Issues:** Graphics card problems can manifest as artifacts on the screen, driver crashes, or no display output.

2. Diagnosing Hardware Problems

- Use diagnostic tools like memtest86+ for RAM testing, CrystalDiskInfo for hard drive health checks, and GPU stress tests for graphics card issues.
- Inspect the physical components for signs of damage or loose connections.

Software Problems

1. Common Software Issues

- **Operating System Errors:** Software conflicts, corrupted system files, or malware infections can cause operating system errors, leading to crashes or instability.
- **Application Crashes:** Individual software applications can crash due to bugs, incompatibility, or conflicts with other software.

2. Diagnosing Software Problems

- Check for software updates, as outdated software can be prone to issues.
- Run antivirus and anti-malware scans to identify and remove malicious software.
- Use system restore points to roll back your system to a previous, stable state if applicable.

Understanding the art of diagnosing common issues is a vital skill on your journey to mastering PC and laptop repair. As we progress through this guide, you'll learn specific techniques for addressing hardware and software problems and effectively bringing your devices back to peak performance.

Atif Shahzad Khan

Chapter 4: Software Troubleshooting

In this chapter, we will delve into the realm of software troubleshooting—a crucial aspect of repairing and maintaining PCs and laptops. We'll explore common software issues that users often encounter and introduce diagnostic and repair software that can aid in identifying and resolving these problems. By mastering these techniques, you'll become adept at keeping your devices running smoothly.

Common Software Issues

1. Operating System Errors

- **Blue Screen of Death (BSOD):** A Windows-specific error screen that appears when the operating system encounters a critical error, typically due to hardware or driver issues.
- **Kernel Panics:** Mac computers display kernel panic screens when the underlying Unix-based macOS encounters a severe error.
- **Linux Kernel Errors:** Similar to BSOD and kernel panics, Linux-based operating systems may display kernel error messages.

2. Application Crashes

- Applications can crash for various reasons, such as software conflicts, compatibility issues, or corrupt configuration files.

Atif Shahzad Khan

3. Startup Problems

- Issues during system startup, like a slow boot process or a system that won't boot at all.

4. Software Conflicts

- Conflicts between different software applications or drivers can lead to instability or crashes.

5. Malware and Viruses

- Malicious software can disrupt system operations, steal data, or render your device unusable.

6. Driver Problems

- Outdated, incompatible, or corrupted device drivers can cause hardware issues and system crashes.

Diagnostic and Repair Software

1. Operating System Diagnostic Tools

- **Windows:** Windows includes built-in diagnostic tools like the Windows Memory Diagnostic for checking RAM, and the System File Checker (SFC) for repairing corrupted system files.
- **macOS:** macOS provides utilities like Disk Utility for checking and repairing disk errors.

Atif Shahzad Khan

- **Linux:** Linux distributions offer various command-line tools and graphical utilities for diagnosing hardware and software issues.

2. Antivirus and Anti-Malware Software

- Robust antivirus and anti-malware software can scan your system for malicious software and remove threats.

3. System Restore

- Many operating systems, including Windows, allow you to create and use system restore points. These snapshots of your system's state can help you revert to a stable configuration when issues arise.

4. Safe Mode

- Booting your system into safe mode loads only essential system files and drivers, helping you identify if third-party software is causing problems.

5. Third-Party Diagnostic Tools

- Various third-party diagnostic tools are available for more in-depth system analysis. Examples include **Malwarebytes** for malware removal and **CCleaner** for system optimization.

Atif Shahzad Khan

6. Driver Update and Management Software

- Tools like **Driver Booster** for Windows and the **Software & Updates** utility in Linux can help you update and manage device drivers.

7. Operating System Repair/Recovery Tools

- Operating system installation media or recovery partitions often contain repair and recovery options, allowing you to fix or reinstall the operating system while preserving your data.

In this chapter, you've been introduced to common software issues that can affect the performance and stability of your PC or laptop. Additionally, we've explored various diagnostic and repair tools available to diagnose and resolve software-related problems. Armed with this knowledge, you'll be well-prepared to tackle a wide range of software issues and keep your devices running smoothly.

Chapter 5: Hardware Replacement and Upgrades

In this chapter, we'll explore the world of hardware replacement and upgrades. Upgrading components like RAM, storage, graphics cards, and CPUs can breathe new life into your PC or laptop, enhance performance, and extend their lifespan. We'll provide step-by-step instructions for each of these common upgrades to empower you to take control of your device's hardware.

Replacing RAM and Storage

Replacing RAM (Random Access Memory)

Step 1: Preparation

- Gather the necessary tools, including a compatible RAM module, a screwdriver (if needed), and an anti-static wrist strap.

Step 2: Shutdown and Safety

- Turn off your computer or laptop and unplug it from the power source. Wear an anti-static wrist strap to protect against ESD.

Step 3: Locate Existing RAM

- Open the case (for desktops) or access the RAM compartment (for laptops). Locate the existing RAM modules.

Step 4: Remove Existing RAM

- Release the retaining clips on the sides of the RAM module to pop it out. Carefully remove it from the slot.

Step 5: Install New RAM

- Align the notches on the new RAM module with those on the slot and gently but firmly press it down until the retaining clips snap into place.

Step 6: Verify Installation

- Close the case (for desktops) or the RAM compartment (for laptops). Power on the device and verify that the new RAM is recognized in the system settings.

Replacing or Upgrading Storage (Hard Drive or SSD)

Step 1: Backup Data

- Before proceeding, ensure you have a backup of your important data.

Step 2: Shutdown and Safety

- Turn off your computer or laptop and unplug it from the power source. Wear an anti-static wrist strap to protect against ESD.

Step 3: Access the Drive

- Open the case (for desktops) or access the storage bay (for laptops) to reach the existing hard drive or SSD.

Step 4: Remove Existing Drive

- Unscrew or release any securing mechanisms holding the existing drive in place. Carefully disconnect cables and remove the drive.

Step 5: Install New Drive

- Connect the new hard drive or SSD and secure it in place. Reconnect cables and secure any screws or brackets.

Step 6: Restore Data

- Restore your data from the backup onto the new storage device.

Step 7: Verify Installation

- Close the case (for desktops) or the storage bay (for laptops). Power on the device and ensure the new drive is recognized in the system settings.

Installing Graphics Cards

Step 1: Preparation

- Gather the necessary tools, including the new graphics card, a screwdriver, and an anti-static wrist strap. Ensure your power supply unit (PSU) can provide adequate power for the new GPU.

Step 2: Shutdown and Safety

- Turn off your computer or laptop and unplug it from the power source. Wear an anti-static wrist strap to protect against ESD.

Step 3: Access the PCIe Slot

- Open the case (for desktops) and locate the PCIe slot where you'll install the graphics card.

Step 4: Remove Existing GPU (if applicable)

- If you're replacing an existing graphics card, carefully unscrew it from the case, disconnect any power connectors, and release any securing mechanisms.

Step 5: Insert New Graphics Card

- Gently insert the new graphics card into the PCIe slot, ensuring it's properly aligned with the slot. Apply even pressure until the card clicks into place.

Step 6: Secure and Connect

- Secure the graphics card by screwing it into the case, and reconnect any power connectors.

Step 7: Driver Installation

- Power on your computer, and install the latest graphics card drivers from the manufacturer's website.

Step 8: Verify Installation

- Confirm that the new graphics card is recognized in the system settings.

Upgrading CPUs

Step 1: Preparation

- Gather the necessary tools, including a compatible CPU, thermal paste, a screwdriver, and an anti-static wrist strap. Ensure your motherboard supports the new CPU.

Step 2: Shutdown and Safety

- Turn off your computer or laptop and unplug it from the power source. Wear an anti-static wrist strap to protect against ESD.

Step 3: Access the CPU Socket

- Open the case (for desktops) and locate the CPU socket on the motherboard.

Step 4: Remove Existing CPU

- Carefully release the CPU socket latch and lift the retaining bracket. Gently remove the existing CPU by lifting it straight up.

Step 5: Install New CPU

- Align the notches on the new CPU with those on the socket and gently lower it into place. Close the retaining bracket and secure it.

Step 6: Apply Thermal Paste

- Apply a small amount of thermal paste onto the CPU, ensuring even coverage.

Step 7: Attach CPU Cooler

- Reattach the CPU cooler, ensuring it's securely fastened and connected to the CPU fan header.

Step 8: Verify Installation

- Close the case (for desktops) and power on the device. Confirm that the new CPU is recognized in the system settings.

In this chapter, we've provided detailed instructions for common hardware upgrades, including RAM and storage replacements, graphics card installations, and CPU upgrades. These hardware enhancements can significantly improve your device's performance and capabilities. As you gain confidence and experience in these processes, you'll have the skills to tailor your PC or laptop to meet your specific needs.

Chapter 6: Preventative Maintenance

Preventative maintenance is the key to keeping your PC or laptop running smoothly and prolonging its lifespan. In this chapter, we'll explore two essential aspects of preventative maintenance: cleaning and dust removal and cooling system maintenance. By incorporating these practices into your routine, you can ensure that your device operates at its best.

Cleaning and Dust Removal

Why Cleaning is Important

Over time, dust and debris accumulate inside your PC or laptop. This buildup can hinder airflow, trap heat, and lead to hardware problems. Regular cleaning is vital to prevent overheating, hardware failure, and performance issues.

Cleaning Supplies

1. Compressed Air: Used to blow dust and debris from components. **2. Soft Bristle Brush:** Ideal for cleaning hard-to-reach areas and vents. **3. Microfiber Cloth:** Used to wipe down surfaces without scratching. **4. Isopropyl Alcohol:** Effective for removing stubborn residue.

Cleaning Steps

Step 1: Shutdown and Disconnect

- Turn off your PC or laptop and unplug it from the power source.

Atif Shahzad Khan

Step 2: Open the Case

- If you have a desktop PC, open the case to access the internal components. For laptops, consult the manufacturer's guide on accessing internals.

Step 3: Blow Out Dust

- Use compressed air to blow dust and debris from components like the CPU heatsink, fans, and power supply. Hold fans in place to prevent them from spinning during cleaning.

Step 4: Brush and Wipe

- Use a soft bristle brush to dislodge stubborn dust and a microfiber cloth dampened with isopropyl alcohol to wipe down surfaces.

Step 5: Reassemble and Test

- Reassemble the PC or laptop, power it on, and ensure it's running smoothly.

Cooling System Maintenance

Why Cooling System Maintenance is Important

The cooling system in your PC or laptop is critical for preventing overheating. Regular maintenance ensures that fans and heatsinks function optimally, which, in turn, extends the life of your components.

Cooling System Maintenance Steps

Step 1: Shutdown and Disconnect

- Turn off your PC or laptop and unplug it from the power source.

Step 2: Open the Case

- If you have a desktop PC, open the case to access the cooling components. For laptops, consult the manufacturer's guide on accessing the cooling system.

Step 3: Cleaning the Fans

- Use compressed air to clean the fans, removing dust and dirt that can obstruct airflow. Hold fans in place to prevent them from spinning during cleaning.

Step 4: Cleaning Heatsinks

- Blow out dust from heatsinks with compressed air, ensuring that they are free from blockages.

Step 5: Reapplying Thermal Paste (Advanced)

- If you have experience or confidence, you can remove the heatsink from the CPU or GPU, clean off old thermal paste, and apply a fresh, thin layer before reattaching it.

Step 6: Reassemble and Test

- Reassemble the PC or laptop, power it on, and monitor the temperatures to ensure they remain within safe limits.

By incorporating regular cleaning and cooling system maintenance into your routine, you'll not only prevent overheating and hardware issues but also prolong the life and performance of your PC or laptop. These practices are essential for a trouble-free computing experience.

Chapter 7: Operating System Installation and Optimization

Installing and optimizing your operating system is a fundamental aspect of maintaining a healthy and efficient PC or laptop. In this chapter, we'll guide you through the process of installing Windows, macOS, or Linux, and provide system optimization tips to enhance your device's performance and responsiveness.

Installing Windows, macOS, or Linux

Installing Windows

Step 1: Prepare Installation Media

- Obtain a bootable Windows installation USB drive or DVD. You can create one using the official Media Creation Tool from Microsoft.

Step 2: Backup Data

- Ensure you have a backup of your important data as the installation process may involve formatting your drive.

Step 3: Boot from Installation Media

- Insert the installation USB drive or DVD into your PC and boot from it. You may need to change the boot order in the BIOS/UEFI settings.

Step 4: Follow Installation Instructions

- Follow the on-screen instructions to select your language, set up your macOS installation location, and configure system preferences.

Step 5: Install and Customize

- Allow the installation to proceed. After completion, you can customize your system settings, create user accounts, and restore data from your backup.

Installing Linux

Step 1: Choose a Distribution

- Select a Linux distribution (e.g., Ubuntu, Fedora, or Debian) and download the installation ISO file.

Step 2: Prepare Installation Media

- Create a bootable Linux installation USB drive using software like Rufus (for Windows) or Etcher (for macOS and Linux).

Step 3: Backup Data

- Backup any critical data on your PC or laptop.

Step 4: Boot from Installation Media

- Insert the installation USB drive and boot from it. You may need to change the boot order in the BIOS/UEFI settings.

Step 5: Follow Installation Wizard

- Follow the on-screen instructions to select your language, time zone, and keyboard layout.

Step 6: Partitioning and Installation

- Configure disk partitions, select the installation location, and create user accounts as prompted.

System Optimization Tips

1. Update Software

- Keep your operating system and software applications up to date to benefit from bug fixes, security patches, and performance improvements.

2. Remove Unnecessary Startup Programs

- Disable or remove programs that launch at startup but aren't essential, as they can slow down your boot time.

Atif Shahzad Khan

3. Disk Cleanup

- Periodically use disk cleanup tools (e.g., Disk Cleanup on Windows, Stacer on Linux) to remove temporary files and free up disk space.

4. Defragment or Optimize Drives

- On Windows, use the built-in Disk Defragmenter tool to optimize hard drives. On Linux, consider using the "fstrim" command for SSDs.

5. Manage Startup Services

- Review and disable unnecessary background services and processes that run on startup to improve system responsiveness.

6. Adjust Visual Effects

- On Windows, you can optimize performance by adjusting visual effects settings to prioritize speed over appearance.

7. Regularly Back Up Your Data

- Implement a regular backup strategy to safeguard your data in case of hardware failures or unexpected data loss.

By following these steps for operating system installation and implementing system optimization tips, you can maintain a well-tuned PC or laptop that delivers optimal performance and a smoother user experience.

Atif Shahzad Khan

Chapter 8: Data Backup and Recovery

Data is the lifeblood of your PC or laptop, and safeguarding it is paramount. In this chapter, we'll explore effective backup strategies to protect your data from loss and outline data recovery methods to help you retrieve lost or corrupted files.

Backup Strategies

Why Backup is Crucial

Data loss can occur due to various reasons, such as hardware failure, accidental deletion, or malware infection. Implementing a reliable backup strategy ensures that your important files are secure and can be easily restored when needed.

Backup Types

1. Full Backups: Full backups copy all data and files from your system to an external drive or cloud storage. This type provides complete data redundancy.

2. Incremental Backups: Incremental backups save only the changes made since the last backup. These backups are more efficient in terms of storage space.

3. Differential Backups: Differential backups save all changes made since the last full backup. While more space-efficient than full backups, they are less efficient than incrementals.

Atif Shahzad Khan

4. Cloud Backups: Cloud-based backup services automatically upload your data to remote servers. They provide offsite data protection and can be accessed from anywhere.

5. Local Backups: Local backups are stored on physical devices like external hard drives or network-attached storage (NAS). They offer quick access but may be vulnerable to local disasters.

Creating a Backup Strategy

1. Identify Critical Data: Determine which files and data are most important to you and need regular backups.

2. Select Backup Locations: Choose where you'll store backups, such as external drives, NAS devices, or cloud services.

3. Backup Frequency: Decide how often you'll perform backups, whether daily, weekly, or in real-time.

4. Backup Software: Use backup software or built-in tools to automate the backup process.

5. Verify Backups: Regularly check that your backups are working correctly and can be restored.

Data Recovery Methods

Data Recovery Software

1. **Deleted File Recovery: Software like Recuva (Windows) and PhotoRec (cross-platform) can recover accidentally deleted files from storage devices.

2. **File Repair Tools: Certain software can repair corrupted files. For example, Microsoft Office includes repair tools for damaged documents.

Backup Restoration

1. **Local Backup: If you have a local backup, restore your data from the backup device using built-in or third-party tools.

2. **Cloud Backup: If you've used a cloud backup service, access the service's interface to retrieve your data.

Professional Data Recovery Services

If you're unable to recover your data using software or backup restoration methods, consider consulting a professional data recovery service. These experts have specialized tools and expertise to recover data from physically damaged drives or severely corrupted storage devices.

Atif Shahzad Khan

Data Recovery Best Practices

1. Act Quickly: If you experience data loss, act promptly to maximize the chances of successful recovery. Avoid using the affected device to prevent overwriting data.

2. Create Disk Images: Before attempting data recovery, create disk images of the affected storage devices to preserve the original state.

3. Label and Organize Backups: Maintain a clear labeling system for your backups, indicating what each backup contains and when it was created.

4. Regularly Test Backups: Periodically restore files from your backups to ensure they are functional.

By implementing a comprehensive backup strategy and understanding data recovery methods, you can safeguard your valuable files and minimize the impact of data loss on your PC or laptop.

Chapter 9: Networking and Internet Connectivity

A robust network connection is essential for a seamless computing experience. In this chapter, we'll delve into troubleshooting common network issues and provide guidance on setting up and securing your Wi-Fi network.

Troubleshooting Network Issues

Identifying Network Problems

1. No Internet Connectivity: If you can't access websites or online services, you may have a problem with your internet connection.

2. Slow Internet: If your internet connection is slow, it could be due to various factors, such as network congestion, hardware limitations, or interference.

3. Intermittent Connectivity: Unpredictable drops in network connectivity can be frustrating. This could result from signal interference, outdated firmware, or router issues.

Troubleshooting Steps

1. Restart Devices: Begin by restarting your modem, router, and computer. This can resolve minor connectivity issues.

2. Check Cables and Connections: Ensure all cables are securely connected, and inspect your network hardware for physical damage.

Atif Shahzad Khan

3. Restart Router: Access your router's web interface and reboot it from there. This can help clear issues within the router.

4. Update Firmware: Ensure your router's firmware is up to date to benefit from performance improvements and security patches.

5. Check for Interference: Identify and eliminate potential sources of interference, such as other electronic devices or neighboring networks.

6. Test Multiple Devices: Confirm whether the issue is isolated to a single device by testing connectivity on multiple devices.

7. Contact ISP: If issues persist, contact your Internet Service Provider (ISP) to check for service interruptions or line issues.

Wi-Fi Setup and Security

Wi-Fi Setup

1. Router Placement: Position your router centrally to ensure even coverage throughout your home or office.

2. SSID and Password: Configure your Wi-Fi network with a unique SSID (network name) and a strong, complex password.

3. Security Type: Use WPA3 or WPA2 encryption to secure your network. Avoid using outdated and vulnerable WEP.

4. Guest Network: Set up a guest network to keep your primary network private and secure.

5. Channel Selection: Use the least congested Wi-Fi channel to minimize interference from neighboring networks.

6. Quality of Service (QoS): Prioritize network traffic for critical devices or applications by configuring QoS settings on your router.

Wi-Fi Security

1. Password Strength: Use a strong, unique password that combines upper and lower-case letters, numbers, and special characters.

2. Regular Password Changes: Change your Wi-Fi password periodically to enhance security.

3. WPS (Wi-Fi Protected Setup): Disable WPS on your router, as it can be vulnerable to brute-force attacks.

4. Firewall and Security Features: Enable firewall and security features on your router to protect against unauthorized access.

5. Firmware Updates: Keep your router's firmware up to date to receive security patches and improvements.

6. Network Monitoring: Regularly review your router's logs for suspicious activity or unauthorized access.

Securing your Wi-Fi network is essential to protect your data and maintain a safe online environment. Additionally, knowing how to troubleshoot network issues ensures that you can quickly address connectivity problems and enjoy a seamless internet experience on your PC or laptop.

Chapter 10: Laptop-Specific Repairs

Laptops are a marvel of portability and convenience, but they can also experience unique issues. In this chapter, we'll explore common laptop-specific repairs, including screen replacement, battery replacement, and keyboard and touchpad repairs. By mastering these repairs, you can extend your laptop's lifespan and save on costly professional services.

Screen Replacement

Why Screen Replacement May Be Necessary

Laptop screens can become damaged due to accidents, impacts, or manufacturing defects. If your laptop's screen displays cracks, dead pixels, or doesn't turn on at all, screen replacement may be required.

Screen Replacement Steps

1. Identify Laptop Model: Determine your laptop's model and screen specifications, including size, resolution, and connector type.

2. Obtain a Replacement Screen: Order a compatible replacement screen from a reputable source.

3. Prepare Workspace: Set up a clean, well-lit workspace with ample room to work.

4. Shutdown and Disconnect: Turn off your laptop, unplug it, and remove the battery (if possible).

5. Remove Bezel and Screen Frame: Carefully pry off the bezel and screen frame, exposing the screen.

6. Detach Old Screen: Disconnect the screen's cables and remove any screws securing it.

7. Install New Screen: Attach the new screen, secure it with screws, and reconnect cables.

8. Test and Reassemble: Power on your laptop to ensure the screen functions correctly. If successful, reassemble the laptop in reverse order.

Battery Replacement

When to Replace the Battery

Laptop batteries degrade over time, resulting in reduced battery life and capacity. If your laptop struggles to hold a charge, discharges quickly, or doesn't turn on without being plugged in, it's time for a battery replacement.

Battery Replacement Steps

1. Identify Laptop Model: Determine your laptop's model and the type of battery it uses (e.g., removable or built-in).

2. Purchase a Replacement Battery: Acquire a compatible replacement battery from a reputable vendor.

3. Shutdown and Disconnect: Turn off your laptop and unplug it.

4. Remove the Old Battery (For Removable Batteries): Release any latches or locks securing the battery, then carefully lift it out.

5. Install the New Battery: Insert the replacement battery and secure it with any latches or locks.

6. Charging and Calibration: Charge the new battery to full capacity and calibrate it as per your laptop manufacturer's instructions.

7. Test: Power on your laptop and ensure the new battery functions correctly.

Keyboard and Touchpad Repairs

Common Keyboard and Touchpad Issues

Laptop keyboards and touchpads can encounter problems such as unresponsive keys, damaged keys, or erratic cursor movement. Repairs may be necessary to restore functionality.

Keyboard and Touchpad Repair Steps

1. Identify the Issue: Determine the specific problem with the keyboard or touchpad.

2. Shutdown and Disconnect: Turn off your laptop and unplug it.

3. Clean the Affected Area: Sometimes, dust and debris can cause issues. Clean the keyboard and touchpad thoroughly.

Atif Shahzad Khan

**4. Keycap Replacement (For Damaged Keys): If a key is damaged, you may need to replace the keycap or the entire keyboard.

**5. Driver Updates (For Touchpad Issues): Update touchpad drivers from the manufacturer's website.

**6. External Keyboard or Mouse: If the built-in keyboard or touchpad is beyond repair, consider using an external keyboard or mouse as a temporary solution.

**7. Professional Repair: If the issue persists, or if you're uncomfortable performing the repair yourself, consult a professional technician for diagnosis and repairs.

By mastering laptop-specific repairs, you can address common issues like screen damage, battery degradation, and keyboard or touchpad malfunctions, effectively extending the life of your laptop and maintaining its functionality.

Chapter 11: Advanced Troubleshooting Techniques

Sometimes, PC and laptop issues go beyond basic repairs and require advanced troubleshooting techniques. In this chapter, we'll explore two critical aspects of advanced troubleshooting: BIOS/UEFI configuration and dealing with boot problems. By mastering these techniques, you can diagnose and resolve complex issues that may arise in your computing devices.

BIOS/UEFI Configuration

Understanding the BIOS/UEFI

The Basic Input/Output System (BIOS) or Unified Extensible Firmware Interface (UEFI) is firmware embedded in your computer's motherboard. It controls hardware settings and the boot process. Accessing and configuring the BIOS/UEFI can help diagnose and resolve hardware-related problems.

Accessing the BIOS/UEFI

1. Restart or Power On: Start or restart your computer.

2. Access Key: During the startup process, a specific key (e.g., F2, Delete, Esc, or F12) is displayed to access the BIOS/UEFI settings. Press this key promptly.

Common BIOS/UEFI Configurations

1. Boot Order: Adjust the boot order to specify which device the computer should boot from first (e.g., hard drive, USB, CD/DVD).

2. Hardware Settings: Configure hardware components like CPU, RAM, and storage devices. Check for any error messages or status indicators.

3. Security Settings: Set BIOS/UEFI passwords for added security.

4. UEFI/BIOS Updates: Check for firmware updates from the motherboard manufacturer's website to resolve compatibility issues or improve stability.

Dealing with Boot Problems

Boot Problem Identification

Boot problems can manifest in various ways, such as a computer that won't start, displays error messages, or repeatedly reboots. Identifying the specific issue is crucial for effective troubleshooting.

Troubleshooting Steps

1. Check Hardware Connections: Ensure all hardware components (CPU, RAM, hard drive/SSD, power cables, etc.) are properly connected.

2. Boot Device Selection: Verify the correct boot device is selected in the BIOS/UEFI settings.

3. Remove External Devices: Disconnect external devices like USB drives, external hard drives, and peripherals and try booting again.

4. Run Diagnostics: Many computers have built-in diagnostics tools accessible through the BIOS/UEFI. Use these tools to identify hardware issues.

5. Safe Mode: Boot your computer into Safe Mode (available in Windows) to troubleshoot software-related problems.

6. Repair Your OS: Use OS repair tools like the Windows Startup Repair utility to fix issues preventing boot.

7. Boot from External Media: If the operating system is corrupt, use installation media (USB or DVD) to access recovery options or reinstall the OS.

8. Test Hardware: If boot issues persist, consider testing hardware components individually, such as RAM, hard drive/SSD, or graphics card.

9. Professional Assistance: If advanced troubleshooting steps don't resolve the issue, consult a professional technician for further diagnosis and repair.

Advanced troubleshooting techniques like accessing and configuring the BIOS/UEFI and addressing boot problems are invaluable when dealing with complex issues that affect your PC or laptop's functionality. By mastering these techniques, you'll be better equipped to handle a wide range of advanced troubleshooting scenarios.

Chapter 12: Resources and References

In the world of PC and laptop repair, knowledge and resources play a crucial role in your success. This chapter provides a valuable list of useful websites and forums, as well as recommended books and courses to help you further enhance your repair skills and stay updated in this ever-evolving field.

Useful Websites and Forums

1. Tom's Hardware (tomshardware.com)

Tom's Hardware is a renowned resource for hardware reviews, guides, and forums where users discuss a wide range of PC and laptop topics, from troubleshooting to hardware upgrades.

2. TechSpot (techspot.com)

TechSpot offers tech news, reviews, and an active community forum. It's a valuable source for troubleshooting guides and hardware-related articles.

3. Linus Tech Tips Forum (linustechtips.com)

Linus Tech Tips is a popular YouTube channel, and their forum is an excellent place to discuss all things related to computers and technology.

4. Reddit - r/techsupport (reddit.com/r/techsupport)

The r/techsupport subreddit is a community of tech enthusiasts and professionals who help answer questions and troubleshoot issues.

5. iFixit (ifixit.com)

iFixit provides detailed repair guides and teardowns for a wide range of electronic devices, including laptops and PCs.

Recommended Books and Courses

1. "CompTIA A+ Certification All-in-One Exam Guide" by Mike Meyers

This book is an excellent resource for individuals looking to earn their CompTIA A+ certification, covering fundamental concepts in PC hardware and software.

2. "Upgrading and Repairing PCs" by Scott Mueller

Scott Mueller's comprehensive book is considered a bible for PC repair technicians. It covers hardware components, troubleshooting, and repair techniques in great detail.

3. Coursera - "Google IT Support Professional Certificate"

This Coursera specialization includes a series of courses covering IT fundamentals, networking, and troubleshooting, which can be beneficial for PC and laptop repair.

4. Udemy - "The Complete Laptop Repair Course"

This Udemy course offers hands-on training in laptop repair, covering topics like hardware replacement, troubleshooting, and maintenance.

5. LinkedIn Learning - Various IT and Hardware Repair Courses

LinkedIn Learning offers a wide range of courses on IT and hardware repair topics, including networking, troubleshooting, and PC maintenance.

Remember to stay up to date with the latest trends and technologies in the PC and laptop repair industry by regularly exploring these resources and continuing your education. Learning and sharing knowledge within the repair community can help you become a more skilled and knowledgeable technician.

Chapter 13: Virus and Malware Removal

Viruses and malware are ever-present threats to the security and performance of your PC or laptop. In this chapter, we'll explore methods for identifying and removing malware, as well as essential tips for preventing infections to keep your devices safe and running smoothly.

Identifying and Removing Malware

Types of Malware

Malware encompasses various malicious software types, including viruses, spyware, adware, ransomware, and more. Identifying the type of malware is crucial for effective removal.

Signs of Malware Infection

1. Sluggish Performance: Noticeably slower system performance, including slow startup and application response times.

2. Unwanted Pop-Ups: Frequent and intrusive pop-up ads, even when browsing safe websites.

3. Changed Browser Settings: Homepage or search engine changes without your consent.

4. Unexplained Data Usage: Sudden spikes in data usage, indicating potential background activity.

Atif Shahzad Khan

5. Disabled Security Software: Malware often disables antivirus or security programs.

Steps for Malware Removal

1. Update Antivirus Software: Ensure your antivirus or anti-malware software is up to date to combat the latest threats.

2. Scan the System: Perform a full system scan to detect and quarantine/remove malware.

3. Quarantine or Remove Malware: Follow the software's prompts to quarantine or remove detected malware.

4. Restart the Computer: Reboot your computer to complete the removal process.

5. Scan Regularly: Schedule regular scans to prevent future infections.

Tips for Preventing Infections

Practice Safe Browsing Habits

1. Keep Software Updated: Regularly update your operating system, web browsers, and software applications to patch security vulnerabilities.

2. Download from Trusted Sources: Only download software and files from reputable sources. Avoid suspicious websites and torrents.

Atif Shahzad Khan

3. Enable Pop-Up Blockers: Use pop-up blockers in your browser to minimize unwanted ads and malicious pop-ups.

4. Exercise Caution with Email Attachments: Avoid opening email attachments from unknown or suspicious senders.

Strengthen Security Measures

1. Install Antivirus Software: Use a reputable antivirus or anti-malware program and keep it up to date.

2. Enable Firewall: Activate your computer's built-in firewall or use a third-party firewall for added protection.

3. Use Strong Passwords: Create complex and unique passwords for your accounts, and consider using a password manager.

4. Enable Two-Factor Authentication (2FA): Activate 2FA for online accounts to add an extra layer of security.

Educate Yourself

1. Stay Informed: Keep up with the latest cybersecurity news and threats to understand potential risks.

2. Be Skeptical: Don't click on suspicious links, download unknown files, or provide personal information to unverified sources.

Atif Shahzad Khan

3. Back Up Data: Regularly back up your important files to an external device or a cloud storage service.

Seek Professional Help

If you suspect a severe malware infection or if your antivirus software can't remove it, consider seeking professional help from a computer technician or a specialized malware removal service.

By following these guidelines for identifying and removing malware and implementing proactive measures to prevent infections, you can significantly reduce the risk of malware compromising your PC or laptop's security and performance.

Atif Shahzad Khan

Chapter 14: Data Security and Privacy

Ensuring the security and privacy of your data is paramount in today's digital age. In this chapter, we'll delve into the importance of data security, the practice of encrypting your data, and secure data disposal techniques. By understanding and implementing these measures, you can safeguard your sensitive information and protect your PC or laptop.

Importance of Data Security

Data Vulnerabilities

Your PC or laptop stores a plethora of sensitive information, including personal documents, financial records, and login credentials. Data vulnerabilities can expose you to various risks, such as identity theft, financial loss, and reputational damage.

Key Aspects of Data Security

1. **Confidentiality: Ensuring that your data remains confidential and only accessible to authorized individuals or entities.

2. **Integrity: Maintaining the accuracy and trustworthiness of your data, protecting it from unauthorized alterations or tampering.

3. **Availability: Ensuring that you can access your data when you need it, without disruptions or downtime.

**4. Compliance: Adhering to data protection laws and regulations applicable in your region.

Encrypting Your Data

What Is Data Encryption?

Data encryption is the process of converting readable data (plaintext) into a scrambled format (ciphertext) that can only be decrypted with the correct decryption key. It provides an added layer of security, making it difficult for unauthorized users to access your sensitive information.

Encrypting Data on Your PC or Laptop

**1. Operating System Encryption: Modern operating systems like Windows and macOS offer built-in encryption tools like BitLocker (Windows) and FileVault (macOS).

**2. Third-Party Encryption Software: You can also use third-party encryption software like VeraCrypt for more advanced encryption options.

**3. Encrypt External Devices: Don't forget to encrypt external storage devices (e.g., USB drives, external hard drives) to protect data on these devices.

**4. Cloud Storage: Consider using cloud storage services that offer end-to-end encryption, such as Tresorit or pCloud.

Secure Data Disposal

Why Secure Data Disposal Matters

When you dispose of your PC or laptop, whether by selling, recycling, or donating, ensuring that your data is thoroughly wiped is essential to prevent it from falling into the wrong hands.

Secure Data Disposal Methods

1. Data Erasure Software: Use specialized data erasure software to securely wipe your hard drive or SSD. Tools like DBAN and Eraser are effective for this purpose.

2. Physical Destruction: Physically destroying the storage device by drilling holes, smashing it, or using a disk shredder ensures data cannot be recovered.

3. Drive Removal: If you're disposing of a desktop PC, consider removing the hard drive or SSD entirely and keeping it secure.

4. Certified Recycling Services: When recycling or donating, use certified recycling services that guarantee secure data disposal.

5. Factory Reset (For Mobile Devices): For mobile devices like smartphones and tablets, perform a factory reset to wipe data before disposal.

Conclusion

Data security and privacy are fundamental in today's digital landscape. By understanding the importance of data security, encrypting your data, and practicing secure data disposal, you can mitigate the risks associated with data breaches and protect your sensitive information on your PC or laptop. Always be proactive in securing your data to maintain peace of mind in an increasingly connected world.

Chapter 15: Troubleshooting Specific Error Messages

Error messages are a common occurrence when using PCs and laptops. They can be frustrating, but they often provide valuable information for diagnosing and resolving issues. In this chapter, we'll explore some common error messages and their solutions to help you troubleshoot and resolve problems effectively.

Common Error Messages and Their Solutions

1. "Blue Screen of Death" (BSOD) Error (Windows)

Error Message: A blue screen with an error message and a stop code (e.g., "PAGE_FAULT_IN_NONPAGED_AREA").

Solution:

- BSOD errors often indicate hardware or driver issues. Restart your computer to see if it resolves the issue.
- Update drivers, especially for graphics cards and other hardware components.
- Check for overheating issues and ensure your computer is adequately cooled.
- Use Windows' built-in memory diagnostic tool to check for RAM problems.
- If problems persist, consult the stop code message for specific troubleshooting steps.

Atif Shahzad Khan

2. "No Bootable Device Found" Error

Error Message: Typically displayed during startup, indicating that the computer cannot find a bootable operating system.

Solution:

- Ensure there are no external devices (e.g., USB drives) connected during startup.
- Check BIOS/UEFI settings to verify the boot order, ensuring the correct boot device is selected.
- Test the hard drive or SSD for errors and replace it if necessary.
- Repair or reinstall the operating system if boot files are corrupted.

3. "Disk Full" or "Low Disk Space" Error

Error Message: Alerts you that your storage drive is running out of space.

Solution:

- Delete unnecessary files and programs to free up space.
- Move large files or media to an external storage device or cloud storage.
- Consider upgrading your storage drive or adding an additional one if space is consistently limited.

Atif Shahzad Khan

4. "File Not Found" or "File Does Not Exist" Error

Error Message: Indicates that a specific file or program cannot be located.

Solution:

- Double-check the file's location or path to ensure it hasn't been moved or deleted.
- Search your computer for the missing file using the built-in search feature.
- Reinstall the software associated with the missing file if necessary.

5. "Internet Connection Lost" Error

Error Message: Informs you that your internet connection has been interrupted.

Solution:

- Check physical connections and reset your modem/router if necessary.
- Restart your computer and reconnect to the network.
- Contact your Internet Service Provider (ISP) if the issue persists.

6. "Access Denied" Error

Error Message: Indicates that you don't have permission to access a specific file or folder.

Solution:

- Check the file or folder's permissions and ownership. Adjust them if needed.
- Ensure you are logged in as an administrator or a user with appropriate permissions.

7. "Critical System Error" (Windows)

Error Message: Typically includes a message like "A critical error has occurred" and may lead to a system restart.

Solution:

- Check for software updates and install any pending Windows updates.
- Scan for malware using antivirus software.
- Examine system logs for more detailed error information.

By understanding these common error messages and their solutions, you'll be better equipped to troubleshoot and resolve issues that may arise while using your PC or laptop. Remember that error messages often contain clues to the underlying problem, so pay close attention to the details provided in the error messages to identify the root cause.

Chapter 16: BIOS/UEFI and Firmware Updates

Your PC or laptop's firmware, including the BIOS (Basic Input/Output System) or UEFI (Unified Extensible Firmware Interface), plays a vital role in its functionality and compatibility. In this chapter, we'll explore the process of updating motherboard firmware and emphasize the importance of keeping firmware up to date.

Updating Motherboard Firmware

What Is BIOS/UEFI Firmware?

The BIOS or UEFI is firmware embedded in your computer's motherboard. It controls essential hardware settings, the boot process, and low-level functions of your PC or laptop.

The Firmware Update Process

1. Identify Your Motherboard: Determine your motherboard's make and model. This information can typically be found in your PC or laptop's documentation or by checking the motherboard itself.

2. Visit the Manufacturer's Website: Go to the website of your motherboard's manufacturer (e.g., ASUS, MSI, Gigabyte) and navigate to the support or downloads section.

3. Locate Firmware Updates: Search for BIOS/UEFI updates specifically designed for your motherboard model. These updates often come in the form of downloadable files.

4. Read Release Notes: Review the release notes associated with the firmware updates. These notes often detail bug fixes, improvements, and new features.

5. Backup Your Data: Before proceeding with a firmware update, it's advisable to back up your important data, as updates can carry risks.

6. Update the Firmware: Download the firmware update file and follow the manufacturer's instructions for updating the BIOS/UEFI. This typically involves running an executable file from a bootable USB drive or directly from the BIOS/UEFI interface.

7. Restart Your Computer: After successfully updating the firmware, restart your PC or laptop to apply the changes.

Caution: Firmware Updates

- **Follow Instructions:** Ensure that you follow the manufacturer's instructions precisely during the update process.
- **Power Interruptions:** Avoid power interruptions during firmware updates, as they can render your motherboard unusable if the update is interrupted.
- **Only When Necessary:** Update firmware only when necessary or when the release notes address specific issues or offer improvements relevant to your system.

Importance of Keeping Firmware Updated

Enhancing Compatibility

Firmware updates often include improvements in hardware compatibility, allowing your PC or laptop to work better with newer components or technologies.

Security Patches

Firmware updates frequently address security vulnerabilities, protecting your system from potential exploits and cyber threats.

Bug Fixes

Updates resolve software and hardware bugs that could cause instability, crashes, or other issues.

Performance Improvements

Firmware updates can improve system performance, boot times, and overall efficiency.

New Features

Some updates introduce new features or options that enhance your computing experience.

Compatibility with Operating Systems

Newer operating systems may require updated firmware to function correctly on your PC or laptop.

Extended Lifespan

Keeping firmware updated can extend the lifespan of your motherboard and other hardware components.

In summary, regularly updating motherboard firmware, including the BIOS/UEFI, is crucial for compatibility, security, performance, and the overall health of your PC or laptop. By following manufacturer guidelines and staying informed about firmware updates, you can ensure your system operates optimally and remains secure.

Chapter 17: Hardware Testing and Diagnostics

The ability to diagnose and test hardware components is essential for effectively troubleshooting PC and laptop issues. In this chapter, we'll explore the use of diagnostic tools and stress testing techniques to identify hardware problems and ensure the reliable performance of your devices.

Using Diagnostic Tools

Diagnostic Tools Overview

Diagnostic tools are software programs specifically designed to assess and report the health and functionality of hardware components in your PC or laptop.

Popular Diagnostic Tools

**1. **Windows Built-In Diagnostic Tools (Windows):

- **Windows Memory Diagnostic:** Checks RAM for errors.
- **Disk Check (Chkdsk):** Scans and repairs file system and disk errors.
- **Device Manager:** Identifies hardware issues, such as driver conflicts.

**2. **Third-Party Diagnostic Tools:

- **Memtest86:** Thoroughly tests RAM for errors and is often used to identify faulty memory modules.

- **CrystalDiskInfo:** Assesses the health of your storage drive, including hard drives (HDDs) and solid-state drives (SSDs).
- **Prime95:** Stress tests CPU and RAM to detect stability issues.
- **FurMark:** Stress tests graphics cards (GPUs) to identify overheating or performance problems.

Running Diagnostic Tools

1. Identify the Problem: Determine which hardware component may be causing the issue. For example, if your computer crashes when running graphics-intensive tasks, focus on testing the GPU.

2. Select the Appropriate Tool: Choose the diagnostic tool that corresponds to the suspected hardware component.

3. Follow the Instructions: Run the tool according to its instructions and wait for results or error reports.

4. Interpret Results: Review the tool's findings. If errors or issues are detected, take appropriate action, such as replacing faulty hardware or updating drivers.

Stress Testing Components

What Is Stress Testing?

Stress testing involves pushing hardware components, such as the CPU, GPU, or RAM, to their limits to determine their stability and performance under heavy loads.

Atif Shahzad Khan

Why Stress Testing Is Important

- **Identify Weaknesses:** Stress tests reveal hardware weaknesses and potential points of failure.
- **Overheating Detection:** Stress testing can uncover overheating problems, which may lead to crashes or system instability.
- **Performance Assessment:** It provides insights into the performance of hardware components under extreme conditions.

Stress Testing Tools

1. Prime95 (CPU and RAM): This tool is often used to stress test CPUs and RAM. It can help detect CPU overheating and memory errors.

2. FurMark (GPU): FurMark is designed for stress testing graphics cards (GPUs) to assess stability and cooling efficiency.

3. HeavyLoad: A versatile stress testing tool that can load CPU, RAM, and hard drives simultaneously.

4. MemTest86: While primarily used for memory diagnostics, it can also be used to stress test RAM by running multiple passes.

5. MSI Kombustor: Useful for testing GPU stability and overclocking limits.

Running Stress Tests

1. Choose the Right Test: Select the appropriate stress test for the hardware component you want to evaluate.

2. Monitor Temperatures: Use hardware monitoring software to keep an eye on component temperatures during the stress test.

3. Run the Test: Start the stress test and let it run for a significant period to assess stability and overheating issues.

4. Interpret Results: Pay attention to any crashes, artifacts, or overheating problems. If issues are detected, take appropriate action, such as adjusting hardware settings or improving cooling.

By mastering the use of diagnostic tools and stress testing techniques, you can efficiently pinpoint hardware problems and assess the overall health and performance of your PC or laptop. Regularly running these tests as part of preventive maintenance can help identify and address issues before they become major problems.

Chapter 18: Soldering and Component-Level Repairs

Soldering and component-level repairs are advanced skills that can be invaluable when fixing PC and laptop issues that involve damaged or malfunctioning electronic components. In this chapter, we'll introduce you to soldering, the essential tools, and the basics of repairing circuit boards.

Introduction to Soldering

What Is Soldering?

Soldering is a technique used to join electronic components or wires by melting solder, a low-temperature metal alloy with a low melting point, typically around 180-190°C (360-375°F). It forms a strong electrical and mechanical bond when it cools and solidifies.

Soldering Tools and Materials

1. Soldering Iron: The primary tool for heating and melting solder. It comes in various wattages, and the tip size can be changed for different soldering tasks.

2. Solder Wire: A roll of solder, typically containing lead-based or lead-free solder alloys. Common diameters are 0.8mm to 1mm.

3. Soldering Station: A more advanced tool that includes temperature control, allowing precise regulation of the soldering iron's heat.

4. Soldering Flux: A chemical substance that aids in soldering by cleaning the surface and preventing oxidation.

5. Desoldering Pump (Solder Sucker): Used to remove old solder or unsolder components.

6. Solder Wick (Desoldering Braid): A copper braid used for desoldering by wicking away molten solder.

7. Third-Hand Tool: A tool with adjustable clamps and magnifying glass to hold components in place during soldering.

Repairing Circuit Boards

Assess the Damage

1. Visual Inspection: Examine the circuit board for signs of damage, such as burnt or loose components, broken traces (conductive pathways), or damaged solder joints.

2. Identify the Problem: Determine which component or connection is causing the issue. This might require testing with a multimeter or observing the circuit's behavior.

Component Replacement

1. Prepare the Workspace: Set up a clean, well-lit workspace with good ventilation. Wear appropriate safety gear, including eye protection.

2. Solder Removal: Use a soldering iron and desoldering pump or solder wick to remove the damaged component or old solder.

3. Component Replacement: Place the new component in the correct orientation and solder it in place. Apply solder to create strong, secure joints.

4. Inspect and Test: Examine the solder joints for quality, ensuring there are no solder bridges (unwanted connections between traces) or cold solder joints (poorly formed joints). Test the repaired circuit to ensure it functions correctly.

Trace Repair

1. Locate the Break: Identify the broken or damaged trace on the circuit board.

2. Clean and Prep: Scrape away any coating or debris covering the trace. Clean the area with isopropyl alcohol.

3. Solder Repair: Use a soldering iron and fine solder wire to bridge the gap in the trace. Ensure the connection is secure and conductive.

4. Test: Verify that the repaired trace restores proper functionality to the circuit.

Safety Precautions

- **Ventilation:** Work in a well-ventilated area or use a fume extractor when soldering to avoid inhaling harmful fumes.
- **Eye Protection:** Wear safety goggles to protect your eyes from solder splatter and debris.
- **Heat Protection:** Use a heat-resistant work surface and keep flammable materials away from your soldering station.
- **Temperature Control:** Adjust your soldering iron to the appropriate temperature for the task to prevent overheating components or damaging the board.

Soldering and component-level repairs require patience, practice, and precision. While they can be incredibly useful for extending the lifespan of electronics and fixing complex issues, they should be approached with care and an understanding of the components and circuitry involved.

Chapter 19: Overheating and Cooling Solutions

Overheating can cause a range of problems in PCs and laptops, including reduced performance and potential damage to internal components. In this chapter, we'll delve into the diagnosis of overheating issues and explore advanced cooling solutions to keep your devices running at optimal temperatures.

Diagnosing Overheating Issues

Signs of Overheating

1. **System Sluggishness: Slower performance and unresponsiveness when running resource-intensive tasks.

2. **Frequent Crashes: Your computer may shut down or restart unexpectedly, especially during demanding tasks.

3. **Loud Fan Noise: Fans working overtime to cool down the system often result in loud noise.

4. **Excessive Heat: Physically touching the laptop or PC case may reveal excessive heat.

Diagnosing Overheating

1. **Monitoring Software: Use monitoring tools like HWMonitor, Core Temp (for CPUs), or MSI Afterburner (for GPUs) to track temperatures.

Atif Shahzad Khan

**2. Check Ventilation: Ensure that the device's vents and fans are clean and unobstructed.

**3. External Factors: Avoid using the laptop or PC on soft surfaces like beds or couches, which can block airflow.

**4. Thermal Paste: Dried or insufficient thermal paste can lead to poor heat transfer from the CPU or GPU to the heatsink.

**5. Hardware Test: Stress test components using tools like Prime95 (CPU) or FurMark (GPU) to see if the device overheats under load.

**6. Check for Dust: Dust buildup inside the device can insulate components and trap heat.

Advanced Cooling Solutions

1. Upgraded Cooling Fans

- Consider installing high-performance cooling fans or coolers, especially in desktop PCs, for improved heat dissipation.

2. Thermal Paste Replacement

- Reapply thermal paste to the CPU and GPU to enhance heat transfer. Clean the old paste thoroughly before applying the new one.

3. Liquid Cooling

- Advanced users can opt for liquid cooling solutions like AIO (All-In-One) coolers or custom loops for efficient and quieter cooling.

4. Overclocking Management

- If you overclock components, ensure that you're not pushing them beyond their safe thermal limits. Monitor temperatures carefully.

5. Laptop Cooling Pads

- Use a laptop cooling pad with built-in fans to help lower the temperature of your laptop during use.

6. Advanced Thermal Design

- High-end PC cases and laptops with superior thermal designs are engineered for improved heat management.

7. Undervolting

- For some laptops, undervolting the CPU and GPU can reduce heat generation without significant performance loss.

8. External Cooling

- In extreme cases, external cooling solutions like external laptop cooling fans or GPU enclosures can be used for enhanced cooling.

9. Proper Cable Management

- Ensure good cable management within your PC case to optimize airflow and reduce heat buildup.

10. Clean Dust Regularly

- Maintain a clean computer by regularly cleaning dust and debris from internal components and fans.

11. Fan Speed Control

- Adjust fan speeds in BIOS/UEFI settings or use third-party software to customize fan profiles for optimal cooling.

12. Optimize System Performance

- Lower graphical settings or resolution in demanding applications or games to reduce heat generation.

Overheating issues can be mitigated and resolved with the right approach. Advanced cooling solutions are often necessary for high-performance systems or when addressing persistent overheating problems. Regular maintenance, proper cooling, and efficient thermal management can extend the life of your PC or laptop and ensure smooth and reliable operation.

Atif Shahzad Khan

Chapter 20: Warranty, Repair Services, and DIY

Understanding warranty coverage, knowing when to seek professional repair services, and recognizing when DIY (Do-It-Yourself) repairs are appropriate are essential aspects of effective PC and laptop maintenance and repair.

Understanding Manufacturer Warranties

What Is a Manufacturer Warranty?

A manufacturer warranty is a guarantee provided by the company that produced your PC or laptop. It outlines the terms and conditions under which the manufacturer will repair or replace faulty components or the entire device within a specified period.

Types of Warranties

1. **Standard Warranty: Most PCs and laptops come with a standard warranty, which typically covers defects in materials and workmanship for one to three years.

2. **Extended Warranty: Extended warranties can be purchased separately, extending the coverage period beyond the standard warranty. They may include additional benefits like accidental damage protection.

Warranty Coverage

1. Inclusions: Manufacturer warranties usually cover manufacturing defects but may exclude accidental damage or normal wear and tear.

2. Duration: Determine the warranty's duration, which can range from one year to several years. Keep track of the warranty expiration date.

3. Conditions: Read the warranty's fine print for conditions that may void coverage, such as unauthorized repairs or physical damage.

4. Transferability: Some warranties are transferable, meaning they remain in effect if you sell or give away the device.

5. Warranty Registration: Some manufacturers require product registration to activate the warranty. Make sure to complete this step if necessary.

6. Proof of Purchase: Keep your purchase receipt or invoice as proof of purchase, which may be required for warranty claims.

Atif Shahzad Khan

When to Seek Professional Repair Services

Signs You Need Professional Repairs

1. **No Warranty: If your warranty has expired or doesn't cover the issue, it's time to consider professional repair services.

2. **Complex Repairs: Complex issues, such as motherboard or screen replacements, typically require professional expertise and specialized equipment.

3. **Safety Concerns: Repairs involving electrical components or soldering should be performed by professionals to ensure safety.

4. **Data Recovery: If you need data recovery services, professionals have the tools and experience to retrieve data from damaged storage devices.

5. **Inadequate DIY Knowledge: If you lack the necessary knowledge or experience to diagnose and repair the problem, it's safer to consult a professional.

6. **Time Constraints: If you require a quick resolution, professional repair services often offer faster turnaround times compared to DIY efforts.

Benefits of Professional Repairs

1. Expertise: Technicians at repair centers have the knowledge and experience to diagnose and fix a wide range of issues.

2. Quality Parts: Reputable repair services use high-quality replacement parts, ensuring reliability.

3. Warranty: Some professional repairs come with a warranty on both parts and labor, providing peace of mind.

4. Safe Repairs: Professionals adhere to safety standards when handling electrical components and hazardous materials.

5. Minimized Risk: Professional repairs reduce the risk of further damage or voiding warranties.

Conclusion

Understanding warranty coverage, recognizing when to seek professional repair services, and knowing when DIY repairs are appropriate are crucial for maintaining your PC or laptop. While DIY repairs can be satisfying and cost-effective for certain issues, professional services ensure quality, safety, and reliability, particularly for complex problems or when warranties are involved. Always consider your specific situation and needs when deciding whether to pursue DIY repairs or consult professionals.

Atif Shahzad Khan

Chapter 21: Troubleshooting Specific Laptop Brands and Models

Different laptop brands and models often come with unique features, designs, and troubleshooting challenges. In this chapter, we'll provide tips for repairing popular laptop brands and offer resources for specific laptop models.

Tips for Repairing Popular Laptop Brands

1. HP (Hewlett-Packard)

- **Common Issues:** Overheating, power-related problems, and graphics card issues.
- **Repair Tips:** Ensure the laptop is clean from dust, update drivers, and check for BIOS/UEFI updates. HP's official website offers comprehensive support resources.

2. Dell

- **Common Issues:** Keyboard and touchpad problems, overheating, and Wi-Fi issues.
- **Repair Tips:** Dell laptops often come with diagnostics tools that can be accessed during boot. Check for hardware issues using these tools. Dell's support website provides detailed troubleshooting guides.

3. Lenovo

- **Common Issues:** Screen flickering, overheating, and hard drive failures.

Atif Shahzad Khan

- **Repair Tips:** Lenovo laptops frequently have built-in diagnostics tools that can be run at startup. You can also find detailed repair guides and drivers on Lenovo's official website.

4. ASUS

- **Common Issues:** Graphics card problems, Wi-Fi connectivity issues, and overheating.
- **Repair Tips:** Use ASUS's built-in diagnostic tools and ensure the laptop is free from dust. ASUS's website offers support resources and driver downloads.

5. Acer

- **Common Issues:** Charging problems, touchpad issues, and overheating.
- **Repair Tips:** Acer laptops often come with recovery tools accessible during boot. Consult Acer's support website for specific guides and drivers.

6. Apple MacBook

- **Common Issues:** Battery and charging problems, keyboard malfunctions, and macOS-related issues.
- **Repair Tips:** If your MacBook is under warranty or AppleCare, consider visiting an Apple Store or authorized service provider. Apple's official support website provides resources for troubleshooting.

7. Microsoft Surface

- **Common Issues:** Screen flickering, touchscreen problems, and battery life concerns.
- **Repair Tips:** If your Surface device is still under warranty, contact Microsoft Support or visit a Microsoft Store. Microsoft's website offers troubleshooting guides and driver updates.

Resources for Specific Laptop Models

1. Manufacturer's Official Websites

- Visit the official website of your laptop's manufacturer for support resources, including drivers, troubleshooting guides, and warranty information.

2. Online Forums and Communities

- Join online forums or communities dedicated to specific laptop brands or models. Users often share experiences and solutions to common problems.

3. YouTube Tutorials

- YouTube hosts a wealth of video tutorials covering laptop repairs, including specific models. Follow step-by-step guides for various issues.

Atif Shahzad Khan

4. Repair Manuals

- Search for repair manuals or service guides for your laptop model. These manuals often provide detailed instructions for disassembly and repair.

5. Laptop Repair Services

- Consider professional laptop repair services or authorized service centers, especially for complex repairs or issues covered under warranty.

6. Manufacturer Support

- Contact the laptop manufacturer's support team for assistance with specific issues or to obtain replacement parts.

When troubleshooting specific laptop brands and models, always refer to manufacturer resources first. These resources are tailored to your device's specifications and provide the most accurate information for repairs and maintenance. Additionally, online communities and tutorials can be valuable sources of insights and solutions for common issues.

Atif Shahzad Khan

Chapter 22: Building Your Own PC

Building your own PC offers the advantage of customization, performance optimization, and potential cost savings compared to pre-built systems. In this chapter, we'll provide a custom PC building guide and tips for choosing compatible components.

Custom PC Building Guide

1. Planning Your Build

- Define your PC's purpose: Gaming, content creation, general use, or specialized tasks.
- Set a budget for your build, considering the cost of components and peripherals.
- Make a list of essential features and components based on your requirements.

2. Choosing Compatible Components

- Ensure compatibility among components (CPU, motherboard, RAM, GPU, storage, power supply, and case).
- Check component sizes and clearances to fit within your chosen case.

3. Selecting Components

- **Central Processing Unit (CPU):**
  - ○ Choose a CPU based on your workload, considering core count, clock speed, and brand preferences (e.g., Intel or AMD).
  - ○ Verify socket compatibility with your chosen motherboard.
- **Motherboard:**
  - ○ Select a motherboard with the right form factor (ATX, Micro-ATX, Mini-ITX) and chipset for your CPU.
  - ○ Check for required features like Wi-Fi, PCIe slots, and RAM capacity.
- **Memory (RAM):**
  - ○ Choose RAM modules with suitable capacity (8GB, 16GB, 32GB) and speed (e.g., DDR4 3200MHz) for your tasks.
  - ○ Ensure compatibility with your motherboard.
- **Graphics Processing Unit (GPU):**
  - ○ Select a GPU based on your graphics requirements (gaming, 3D rendering, video editing).
  - ○ Verify that your power supply can support the GPU's power needs.
- **Storage:**
  - ○ Combine SSDs for fast boot and application load times with HDDs for mass storage if needed.
  - ○ Consider NVMe M.2 SSDs for faster data transfer speeds.

Atif Shahzad Khan

- **Power Supply Unit (PSU):**
  - Calculate your power requirements and choose a PSU with sufficient wattage (consider future upgrades).
  - Opt for a reliable, reputable brand to ensure stable power delivery.
- **Case:**
  - Pick a case that accommodates your components and provides good airflow.
  - Choose a design and size that fits your aesthetic preferences.
- **Cooling:**
  - Stock CPU coolers are sufficient for most users. If overclocking or better cooling is needed, consider an aftermarket cooler.
- **Operating System:**
  - Decide on the operating system (e.g., Windows, Linux) and purchase a valid license.

4. Assembling Your PC

- **Work in an ESD-safe environment:** Avoid static electricity by working on an anti-static mat or using an ESD wrist strap.
- **Follow the motherboard manual:** Step-by-step instructions are usually included.
- **Install components in the following order:** CPU, RAM, GPU, storage drives, PSU, and cable management.
- **Apply thermal paste:** A small amount helps with heat transfer between the CPU and cooler.

- **Cable management:** Keep cables organized for better airflow and aesthetics.

5. First Boot and Setup

- **First boot:** Power on your PC and ensure all components are functioning correctly.
- **BIOS/UEFI setup:** Access the BIOS/UEFI to configure boot order and check component recognition.
- **Install the operating system:** Use a bootable USB drive to install the OS and required drivers.

6. Driver Installation and Updates

- **Download and install drivers:** Visit the manufacturer's websites for the latest drivers for your components.
- **Windows Update:** Keep your operating system up to date with the latest security patches and updates.

7. Testing and Benchmarking

- **Stress test:** Use software like Prime95 and FurMark to stress test CPU and GPU stability.
- **Benchmark:** Run benchmark tools like 3DMark or Cinebench to assess system performance.

8. Maintenance and Upgrades

- Regularly clean dust from components and fans.
- Monitor temperatures and hardware health.
- Consider upgrades for improved performance when needed.

Atif Shahzad Khan

Conclusion

Building your own PC can be a rewarding and cost-effective way to have a customized, high-performance system. Careful planning, component selection, and attention to detail during assembly are essential for a successful build. Whether for gaming, productivity, or content creation, custom PC building allows you to create a machine that perfectly suits your needs and preferences.

Chapter 23: Future Trends in PC and Laptop Repair

As technology continues to advance at a rapid pace, the world of PC and laptop repair faces new challenges and opportunities. In this chapter, we'll explore emerging technologies and the repair challenges they present.

Emerging Technologies and Repair Challenges

1. Miniaturization and Integration

- **Challenge:** As components become smaller and more integrated, diagnosing and repairing specific parts may become increasingly difficult without specialized tools.

2. Soldered Components

- **Challenge:** The soldering of components directly onto the motherboard (e.g., RAM, storage) can limit repairability, requiring entire motherboard replacements for minor issues.

3. Modular Design

- **Opportunity:** Some manufacturers are moving towards more modular designs, allowing for easier component replacement and upgrades.

Atif Shahzad Khan

4. Thin and Lightweight Laptops

- **Challenge:** Ultrathin laptops with limited internal space may be more challenging to repair due to compact layouts and components.

5. Battery Advancements

- **Challenge:** While longer-lasting batteries are beneficial, some designs incorporate glued or sealed battery units that are challenging to replace.

6. Advanced Cooling Systems

- **Challenge:** Complex cooling solutions, such as vapor chamber cooling and multiple fans, require specialized knowledge for maintenance and repair.

7. Component Authentication and Lockdown

- **Challenge:** Some manufacturers are implementing hardware authentication to prevent third-party repairs, potentially limiting options for independent repair technicians.

8. AI and Machine Learning

- **Opportunity:** AI-driven diagnostic tools may assist in pinpointing hardware and software issues quickly, streamlining the repair process.

9. Advanced Connectivity

- **Challenge:** The proliferation of various connectivity standards (USB-C, Thunderbolt, Wi-Fi 6, 5G) can lead to compatibility issues and require advanced troubleshooting.

10. Biometric Security

- **Challenge:** Devices with biometric security features like facial recognition may require specialized repair techniques to maintain user privacy and security.

11. Wearable Technology and IoT Integration

- **Challenge:** Wearables and IoT devices are becoming more integrated with traditional PCs and laptops. Repair technicians may need broader expertise to address these interconnected systems.

12. Quantum Computing

- **Future Challenge:** Quantum computers, once more prevalent, will introduce entirely new hardware paradigms, necessitating specialized repair knowledge.

13. Sustainability and Eco-Friendly Design

- **Opportunity:** Manufacturers are increasingly focused on eco-friendly and repairable designs, promoting a longer lifespan for devices.

Atif Shahzad Khan

14. Virtual and Augmented Reality

- **Challenge:** Repairing VR and AR headsets and peripherals may require specialized knowledge due to their unique components and technologies.

15. Cybersecurity Concerns

- **Challenge:** Repairing and securing devices against emerging cybersecurity threats will become even more critical in the future.

Conclusion

The world of PC and laptop repair is ever-evolving, driven by emerging technologies and evolving design trends. While these changes present new challenges, they also offer opportunities for innovation and specialization within the repair industry. Repair technicians must stay informed about these trends and continuously update their skills to meet the demands of repairing the next generation of computing devices. As technology continues to advance, the future of PC and laptop repair promises exciting and dynamic opportunities.

Chapter 24: Troubleshooting Resources and Tools

Successful troubleshooting often depends on access to the right resources and tools. In this chapter, we'll provide a detailed list of useful resources and tools for diagnosing and repairing PC and laptop issues.

Troubleshooting Resources

1. Manufacturer's Websites

- Access official support websites for your device's manufacturer to find drivers, manuals, and troubleshooting guides.

2. Online Forums and Communities

- Join forums like Reddit's r/techsupport or Tom's Hardware to seek advice from experienced users and professionals.

3. Tech Support Websites

- Explore dedicated tech support websites such as TechSpot, BleepingComputer, or the official Microsoft Support.

4. YouTube Tutorials

- YouTube hosts a vast library of video tutorials covering various repair and troubleshooting topics.

Atif Shahzad Khan

5. Official Documentation

- Refer to official documentation, including user manuals and service guides, often available on the manufacturer's website.

6. Diagnostic Software

- Use built-in diagnostic tools in your operating system or third-party software like HWMonitor, CrystalDiskInfo, and MemTest86.

7. Troubleshooting Books

- Consider books like "Troubleshooting and Repairing Laptops" by Scott Mueller for in-depth repair guidance.

Troubleshooting Tools

1. Screwdriver Set

- A precision screwdriver set is essential for opening laptops and PCs.

2. ESD Protection

- Invest in an anti-static wrist strap or anti-static mat to prevent electrostatic discharge during repairs.

3. Multimeter

- A digital multimeter is useful for measuring voltage, resistance, and continuity in electronic components.

4. Soldering Iron

- For soldering and component-level repairs, a good-quality soldering iron is indispensable.

5. Desoldering Tools

- Tools like solder wick and desoldering pumps help remove solder during repairs.

6. Cable Tester

- Useful for verifying cable integrity and identifying faulty connections.

7. Diagnostic Software

- Software tools like Prime95, FurMark, and MemTest86 assist in hardware diagnostics.

8. Bootable USB Drive

- Create bootable USB drives with diagnostic tools and operating system installation files.

Atif Shahzad Khan

9. Cable Management Tools

- Cable ties, Velcro straps, and cable organizers help maintain a tidy interior for improved airflow.

10. Heat Sink Compound

sql
- Used for reapplying thermal paste when cooling components like the CPU or GPU.

11. Data Recovery Tools

python
- Data recovery software like Recuva or TestDisk can help recover lost data from storage devices.

12. External Drive Enclosure

csharp
- Useful for connecting and recovering data from removed storage drives.

13. USB Drive with Portable Apps

csharp
- Create a USB drive loaded with portable diagnostic and repair utilities for on-the-go troubleshooting.

14. External Monitor/Keyboard/Mouse

diff
- Handy for testing laptop displays, keyboards, and trackpads during repairs.

15. Network Cable Tester

diff

- Essential for diagnosing network connectivity issues.

16. Flashlight and Magnifying Glass

diff

- Helpful for inspecting small components and PCBs.

17. Computer Repair Toolkits

diff

- Pre-assembled toolkits often include essential screwdrivers, spudgers, and other tools.

Conclusion

Having access to a comprehensive set of resources and tools is crucial for efficient troubleshooting and successful PC and laptop repairs. Whether you're diagnosing hardware issues, recovering data, or conducting component-level repairs, a well-equipped toolkit and knowledge of available resources can make the troubleshooting process more manageable and effective. Stay up-to-date with the latest tools and resources to keep your repair skills sharp in the ever-evolving world of technology.

Chapter 25: Real-Life Repair Stories and Case Studies

Learning from real-life repair stories and case studies can provide valuable insights into common issues, solutions, and lessons learned in the world of PC and laptop repair. In this chapter, we'll share stories of successful repairs and the lessons gained from them.

Stories of Successful Repairs

Case Study 1: Overheating Laptop

Issue: A customer brought in a laptop that was shutting down unexpectedly and displaying graphical glitches. The laptop's bottom felt extremely hot during use.

Solution: After disassembling the laptop and removing accumulated dust from the cooling system, it was clear that the overheating was causing the problems. We replaced the dried-out thermal paste, cleaned the heatsinks and fans, and reassembled the laptop. It ran smoothly without overheating or graphical glitches.

Lesson: Overheating is a common issue in laptops, often caused by dust accumulation and degraded thermal paste. Regular cleaning and maintenance can extend a laptop's life.

Case Study 2: Non-Booting PC

Issue: A desktop PC wouldn't power on at all, despite multiple attempts. No fans or lights were working.

Atif Shahzad Khan

Solution: We started by checking the power source and confirmed it wasn't the issue. Upon closer inspection, we found a loose internal power connector that had disconnected from the motherboard. Reconnecting it solved the problem, and the PC booted successfully.

Lesson: Sometimes, seemingly catastrophic failures can have simple solutions. Always check for loose connections before assuming the worst.

Case Study 3: Data Recovery from a Dead Hard Drive

Issue: A customer's laptop had a failed hard drive, rendering it unbootable. The customer had valuable data on the drive and wanted it recovered.

Solution: We removed the hard drive and placed it in an external drive enclosure. While the drive was no longer usable as a boot drive, we were able to access the data and back it up to another storage device.

Lesson: Data recovery is possible even from failed drives if you handle them carefully and use the right tools.

Lessons Learned from Repairing PCs and Laptops

**1. Regular Maintenance Matters

- The first line of defense against many issues is regular maintenance, including cleaning out dust and debris, updating drivers, and applying fresh thermal paste.

**2. Check the Basics First

- Before delving into complex diagnostics, ensure that power sources and connections are secure.

**3. Back Up Your Data

- Data loss is a common concern. Regularly back up your important files to prevent catastrophic data loss in case of hardware failure.

**4. **Take Precautions with Static Electricity

- Always use ESD protection when working with sensitive electronic components to avoid damage from electrostatic discharge.

**5. **Don't Overlook the Power of Simple Solutions

- Some of the most frustrating issues can have straightforward fixes. Start with the basics before assuming the worst.

**6. **Experience Is a Great Teacher

- Real-world repair experiences teach valuable lessons that go beyond theory. Learn from each repair case to become a more skilled technician.

**7. **Data Recovery Is Possible

- Even in the face of failing hardware, data recovery is often feasible with the right tools and methods.

Conclusion

Real-life repair stories and case studies provide insights into the world of PC and laptop repair that go beyond theory. Whether it's resolving overheating issues, fixing loose connections, or recovering data from a dead drive, every repair case offers valuable lessons. These stories remind us of the importance of regular maintenance, troubleshooting fundamentals, and the power of simple solutions in the world of technology repairs.

Chapter 26: Reader's Q&A and Troubleshooting Solutions

In this chapter, we'll address common questions from readers and share success stories submitted by individuals who applied troubleshooting solutions learned from this guide.

Answering Common Questions from Readers

Question 1: What Should I Do If My Laptop Gets Wet?

Answer: If your laptop gets wet, turn it off immediately, unplug it, and remove the battery (if possible). Let it dry thoroughly for at least 48 hours in a cool, dry place. Do not use a hairdryer or heat source, as this can damage components. After drying, if the laptop doesn't work, seek professional repair.

Question 2: My Laptop Keeps Overheating. What Can I Do?

Answer: Overheating can be caused by dust accumulation or degraded thermal paste. Open your laptop, clean out dust, and replace the thermal paste on the CPU and GPU. Ensure the cooling system is functioning correctly and consider using a laptop cooling pad.

Question 3: How Can I Recover Data from a Dead Hard Drive?

Answer: If the hard drive is no longer recognized, consider using a data recovery service. If it's still recognized but won't boot, you can remove the drive, connect it to another computer using an external enclosure, and attempt data recovery using software like Recuva or TestDisk.

Question 4: What Should I Do If My PC Won't Boot After a Windows Update?

Answer: If a Windows update causes boot issues, you can try booting into Safe Mode and rolling back the update. If that doesn't work, create a bootable Windows USB drive, boot from it, and attempt a repair or reinstall. Always back up important data before making significant changes.

Sharing Reader Success Stories

Success Story 1: Screen Replacement

Reader: John S.

Story: My laptop's screen had a large crack, rendering it unusable. I followed the guide in this ebook for screen replacement, ordered a compatible replacement screen, and carefully swapped it out. It took some time and patience, but the laptop is now working perfectly with a brand new screen.

Lesson: Replacing a laptop screen is challenging but achievable with the right resources and careful execution.

Atif Shahzad Khan

Success Story 2: Data Recovery

Reader: Emily T.

Story: I accidentally deleted important documents from my external hard drive. I was devastated until I read the data recovery chapter in this ebook. I followed the steps, used data recovery software, and managed to recover all my lost files. Thank you!

Lesson: Data recovery software can work wonders when it comes to retrieving accidentally deleted files.

Success Story 3: Overheating Fix

Reader: Michael R.

Story: My gaming laptop was overheating and throttling performance during gaming sessions. After reading the overheating chapter in this guide, I disassembled the laptop, cleaned the dust, and applied new thermal paste. Now, it runs much cooler, and my gaming experience has improved significantly.

Lesson: Overheating laptops can often be fixed with thorough cleaning and new thermal paste application.

Conclusion

Reader questions and success stories demonstrate the practical value of the knowledge shared in this guide. Whether it's addressing common issues like overheating, data recovery, or screen replacement, the solutions presented here empower readers to tackle their own repair challenges with confidence. Learning from each other's experiences enriches the world of PC and laptop repair.

Atif Shahzad Khan

Chapter 27: Additional Tips and Tricks

Efficiency and time-saving techniques can make a significant difference in the world of PC and laptop repair. In this chapter, we'll share valuable tips and tricks to help you maximize your efficiency in repairs.

Time-Saving Techniques

**1. Label and Organize

- Use adhesive labels or masking tape to mark cables and connectors before disassembly. This makes reassembly quicker and reduces the chance of mistakes.

**2. Create a Workspace Checklist

- Before starting a repair, create a checklist of tools and components you'll need. This prevents frequent trips to your toolbox and helps you stay organized.

**3. Digital Documentation

- Take photos or videos of the disassembly process, especially if you're dealing with a complex repair. You can reference these visuals during reassembly.

**4. Group Similar Repairs

- If you're repairing multiple devices of the same type (e.g., laptops or desktops), group them together. This allows you to streamline the repair process by addressing similar issues at once.

**5. Use Magnetic Screw Trays

- Magnetic trays keep screws organized and prevent them from rolling away. You won't waste time searching for lost screws.

**6. **Pre-Test After Repairs

- Before fully reassembling a device, do a quick pre-test to ensure it functions as expected. This saves time by avoiding the need to disassemble and diagnose again.

Maximizing Efficiency in Repairs

**1. Practice Diagnostics

- Hone your diagnostic skills to quickly identify the root cause of a problem. A precise diagnosis leads to efficient repairs.

**2. Invest in Quality Tools

- Quality tools may cost more upfront, but they can save you time and frustration in the long run.

Atif Shahzad Khan

**3. **Keep Common Parts on Hand

- Maintain a stock of common replacement parts (e.g., RAM, storage drives, power supplies) to avoid delays in waiting for orders.

**4. **Stay Updated

- Regularly update your knowledge about new hardware, software, and repair techniques. Being up-to-date reduces troubleshooting time.

**5. **Work in a Clean Environment

- A clean workspace reduces the chances of accidents, misplacements, or damage to components.

**6. **Prioritize Safety

- Always prioritize safety, especially when dealing with electrical components. This includes disconnecting power sources and using ESD protection.

**7. **Learn Keyboard Shortcuts

- Become proficient with keyboard shortcuts in operating systems and software tools to navigate faster.

**8. **Keep Repair Records

- Maintain a log of your repair activities, including what issues were resolved and what components were replaced. This helps in future diagnostics.

**9. **Use Online Resources

- Online repair manuals, forums, and communities can provide quick solutions to common issues you encounter.

**10. **Network with Other Technicians

csharp

- Building relationships with other technicians can be a valuable resource for sharing tips, insights, and troubleshooting solutions.

Conclusion

Efficiency in PC and laptop repair comes from a combination of well-honed techniques, organization, quality tools, and continuous learning. Whether you're working as a professional technician or performing repairs as a hobby, these tips and tricks will help you save time and increase your effectiveness. A well-organized and efficient approach to repairs not only benefits you but also ensures timely solutions for your clients or personal devices.

Chapter 28: Building a PC Repair Business

Starting a PC repair business can be a rewarding venture for those with technical skills and a passion for helping others with their technology issues. In this chapter, we'll provide tips for launching your PC repair business and managing marketing and customer relations.

Tips for Starting a PC Repair Business

**1. Assess Your Skills

- Ensure you have a strong foundation in PC and laptop repair, including hardware and software troubleshooting. Consider getting certified to build credibility.

**2. Business Plan

- Create a comprehensive business plan outlining your services, target market, pricing, and growth strategy. Having a plan is crucial for long-term success.

**3. Legal Considerations

- Register your business and obtain any necessary licenses or permits. Consult with a legal professional to structure your business appropriately.

Atif Shahzad Khan

**4. Tools and Equipment

- Invest in quality tools and equipment needed for repairs. Having reliable tools ensures efficient and professional service.

**5. Stock Replacement Parts

- Maintain an inventory of commonly used replacement parts (e.g., RAM, hard drives, power supplies) to avoid delays in completing repairs.

**6. Service Area

- Determine your service area. Will you offer on-site repairs, remote support, or both? Define your geographic coverage.

**7. Pricing Strategy

- Establish competitive pricing for your services. Consider offering flat-rate fees for common repairs to simplify billing.

**8. Marketing

- Develop a strong online presence with a professional website and active social media profiles. Consider online advertising and local SEO to reach potential customers.

Atif Shahzad Khan

**9. Customer Relations

- Provide excellent customer service. Be responsive, communicate clearly, and ensure customers are satisfied with your work.

**10. Warranties and Guarantees

vbnet
- Offer warranties on your repairs to build trust with customers. Be clear about what is covered and for how long.

**11. Network with Local Businesses

vbnet
- Establish partnerships with local businesses, such as computer retailers or office supply stores, to gain referrals.

**12. Feedback and Improvement

css
- Encourage feedback from customers and use it to improve your services. Positive reviews can be valuable for your reputation.

Marketing and Customer Relations

**1. Online Presence

- Create a professional website with information about your services, pricing, contact details, and customer testimonials.

**2. Social Media

- Maintain active social media profiles, posting tips, tech news, and promotions to engage with potential customers.

**3. Local SEO

- Optimize your website for local search engine results to ensure your business appears when people search for PC repair services in your area.

**4. Online Advertising

- Consider pay-per-click (PPC) advertising on platforms like Google Ads and social media to reach a wider audience.

**5. Customer Referral Program

- Implement a referral program to incentivize existing customers to refer others to your business.

**6. Email Marketing

- Collect customer email addresses and send regular newsletters with tech tips, special offers, and updates about your business.

Atif Shahzad Khan

**7. Prompt Communication

- Respond to inquiries and service requests promptly. Clear and timely communication builds trust.

**8. Customer Education

- Educate customers about proper maintenance and data backup practices to reduce the need for future repairs.

**9. Quality Service

- Focus on delivering high-quality repairs and exceptional customer experiences. Satisfied customers are more likely to refer others.

**10. Follow-Up

python
- Follow up with customers after repairs to ensure everything is working correctly and address any additional questions or concerns.

Conclusion

Starting and growing a successful PC repair business requires technical expertise, effective marketing, and exceptional customer relations. By following these tips and strategies, you can build a reputation for reliable and professional service, attract a loyal customer base, and position your business for long-term success in the competitive tech repair industry.

Atif Shahzad Khan

Conclusion

Congratulations! You've embarked on a journey to master the art of PC and laptop repair. In this comprehensive guide, we've covered everything from the fundamentals of hardware and software to advanced troubleshooting techniques, and we've explored the intricacies of building and growing a successful repair business. As we wrap up, let's reflect on what you've learned and encourage you to continue your exploration in the ever-evolving world of technology.

Final Thoughts and Encouragement

Throughout this guide, you've gained valuable insights into the inner workings of computers and laptops. You've learned to diagnose and fix common issues, recover data, and even start your own repair business. Remember that knowledge is power, and your newly acquired skills have the potential to benefit you in many ways, whether personally or professionally.

Encouraging Readers to Continue Learning and Exploring

The world of technology is constantly evolving, and there will always be more to learn and explore. New hardware and software technologies, emerging trends, and innovative repair techniques continue to shape the industry. Embrace the excitement of learning, stay curious, and remain adaptable to change.

Atif Shahzad Khan

Recap of Key Points

- **Understanding Hardware and Software:** You've gained a deep understanding of the components that make up a PC or laptop and learned how to troubleshoot both hardware and software issues.
- **Advanced Troubleshooting:** You've honed your diagnostic skills and can confidently tackle complex issues, from overheating problems to data recovery.
- **Business Success:** If you've considered starting a PC repair business, you've discovered the essential steps for success, from planning and legal considerations to marketing and customer relations.
- **Efficiency and Customer Satisfaction:** You've learned the value of efficiency in repairs and how to provide exceptional customer service, ensuring satisfied clients and positive word-of-mouth.

Encouragement for Readers

As you move forward in your journey, remember that every challenge you encounter is an opportunity to learn and grow. Mistakes are stepping stones to success, and each repair, whether successful or challenging, contributes to your expertise. Stay patient, persistent, and open to new technologies.

Whether you're helping a friend revive their aging laptop, launching your own repair business, or simply satisfying your curiosity about the intricate world of technology, your knowledge and skills are invaluable. Continue to seek out

Atif Shahzad Khan

resources, ask questions, and share your knowledge with others. The journey of mastering PC and laptop repair is a rewarding one, and it's a journey that never truly ends.

So, as you venture forth, may your tools remain sharp, your diagnostics clear, and your passion for technology repair burn brightly. With every repair, you're not just fixing devices; you're enabling people to stay connected, productive, and empowered in the digital age. Happy repairing, and may your journey be filled with success, innovation, and endless possibilities.

Atif Shahzad Khan

Appendix

Glossary of Technical Terms

In the world of PC and laptop repair, technical jargon is common. This glossary provides definitions for key terms used throughout this guide:

- **BIOS (Basic Input/Output System):** The firmware that initializes hardware during the boot process and provides a low-level interface for configuring hardware settings.
- **CPU (Central Processing Unit):** The primary processing unit of a computer that executes instructions and performs calculations.
- **RAM (Random Access Memory):** Temporary storage that holds data and instructions while the CPU processes them.
- **GPU (Graphics Processing Unit):** A specialized processor designed for rendering graphics and images.
- **SSD (Solid-State Drive):** A storage device that uses NAND flash memory to store data, providing faster data access compared to traditional hard drives.
- **HDD (Hard Disk Drive):** A storage device that uses spinning magnetic disks to store data.
- **Motherboard:** The main circuit board of a computer, containing the CPU, RAM, and various connectors for peripherals.
- **Operating System:** Software that manages hardware resources, provides user interfaces, and allows applications to run.

Atif Shahzad Khan

- **Driver:** Software that enables communication between hardware devices and the operating system.
- **BIOS/UEFI Update:** Updating the firmware that controls the motherboard's functions, including booting and hardware configuration.
- **Thermal Paste:** A heat-conductive compound applied between the CPU/GPU and their heatsinks to improve heat transfer.
- **Data Backup:** Creating copies of important files and data to prevent loss in case of hardware failure or data corruption.
- **Malware:** Malicious software, including viruses, spyware, and ransomware, designed to harm or steal data.
- **ESD (Electrostatic Discharge):** A sudden discharge of static electricity that can damage electronic components.
- **Network Connectivity:** The ability of a device to connect to a network, including wired and wireless connections.
- **BIOS/UEFI Configuration:** Adjusting settings in the motherboard's firmware to control boot order and hardware behavior.
- **Diagnostic Tools:** Software and hardware tools used to identify and troubleshoot hardware and software issues.
- **Component-Level Repairs:** Repairs that involve replacing or fixing individual hardware components on a circuit board.

Troubleshooting Flowcharts

Flowcharts provide step-by-step guidance for diagnosing and resolving common PC and laptop issues. Refer to these flowcharts when faced with specific problems to streamline your troubleshooting process.

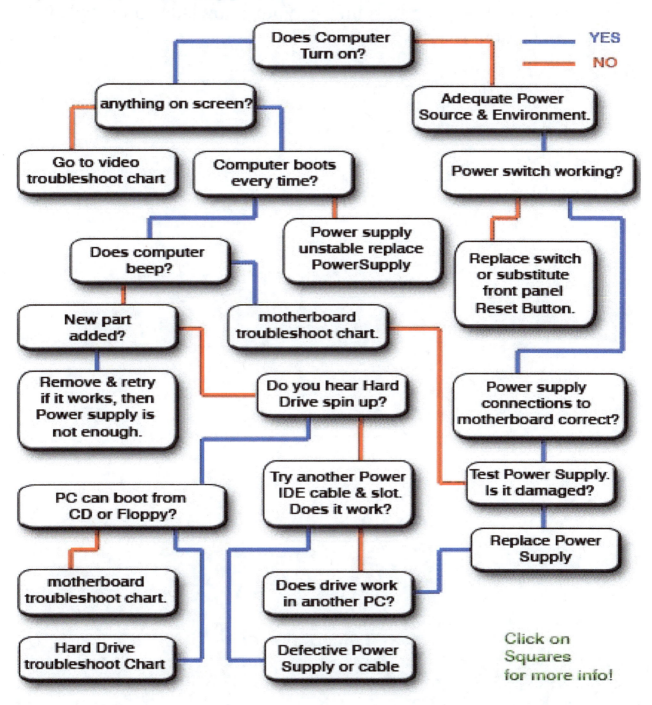

The appendix contains valuable resources to enhance your understanding of technical terms, streamline troubleshooting processes, and access quick reference guides for various repair procedures. Use these resources as a companion to the main content of this guide to reinforce your knowledge and skills in PC and laptop repair.

Atif Shahzad Khan